How Plants Travel

Joan Elma Rahn

Illustrated by Ginny Linville Winter

Atheneum   1973   New York

To Kendall Winter

Text copyright © 1973 by Joan E. Rahn
Illustrations copyright © by Ginny L. Winter
All rights reserved
Library of Congress catalog card number 73-76332
ISBN 0-689-30118-9
Published simultaneously in Canada by
McClelland & Stewart, Ltd.
Manufactured in the United States of America
Printed by Halliday Lithograph Corporation
Bound by A. Horowitz & Son/Bookbinders
Clifton, New Jersey
Designed by Harriett Barton
First Edition

Rahn, Joan Elma
  How plants travel. Illus. by Ginny
Linville Winter. Atheneum 1973
  58p illus

1. Plants I

CATALOG CARD

(11/23/82)

≥ 9 1980

AUG 7 1981

How Plants Travel

Contents

How Plants Travel

Introduction

Plants travel. Every year, I pull dandelions out of my lawn, but no one ever planted dandelions there.

Another part of my lawn has received no care for several years. Today, many plants besides grass and dandelions grow there: asters, goldenrods, bittersweet nightshade, sow thistle, elder bushes, and even some young horse chestnut trees.

Where did they come from? Mostly from seeds or fruits produced by plants of the same kind in my neighbors' yards or along the roadsides.

During World War II, the German planes that bombed London set many fires. Later, fireweeds appeared in the burned-over areas. Londoners, who never had seen these plants before, wondered where they had come from. They had grown from seeds blown by the winds from fireweeds growing in the countryside. In the city, some of the seeds landed on burned ground, which is one of the most suitable places for fireweeds.

In 1861, a Frenchman exploring in the jungles of Cambodia discovered an ancient city called Angkor. Five hundred years before, the inhabitants of Angkor had abandoned their city. With no one to care for them, the roads and buildings soon became covered with vines and other plants. These were the offspring of plants living in the nearby jungles.

Coconut palm trees grow on the beaches of the Hawaiian Islands, and ferns and other plants cover the hillsides. These islands once had no plants, for Hawaii was formed from volcanoes that rose from the bottom of the sea and then sent fiery lava down their sides. So hot was the lava that nothing could live there. When the lava cooled, the islands consisted of only barren rock, but today they bear beautiful forests. Hawaiian plants came to the islands by long journeys. Winds and ocean currents carried some of them from distant lands. Later, when people came to the islands, they brought more plants with them from their homelands.

Do you ever see evidence that plants travel? Have you observed young maple or elm trees growing in a gravel driveway that once had no plants?

Do you or your parents have to pull weeds from a vegetable garden?

Is one of your neighbors careless about cleaning the gutters of his house? If so, do seedlings sprout there?

Have you ever seen mosses or lichens growing on very old gravestones?

The more you look about you, the more you will see plants growing where once they did not grow. In each case, a plant or part of a plant came to that spot from some other place. Perhaps, it traveled only a few inches, or its journey may have covered thousands of miles.

The Advantages of Traveling

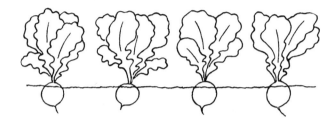

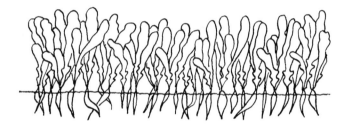

Did you ever have a vegetable garden? The directions on a package of radish seeds tell you to plant them about a quarter of an inch apart. Then, after the seedlings appear and have grown a little, you are to transplant them so that they are about 2 inches apart. If you didn't do this, the radish seedlings would be much too crowded. They would shade each other, and none would have enough light to grow into sturdy, healthy plants. In dry weather, there would not be enough water for all of them, and many would wilt and die. Perhaps none of them would ever produce a radish.

If all the seeds of a tree were to fall directly beneath it, the same kind of thing would happen. Probably, none of the young trees from these seeds would become large enough to produce its own seeds. This is one reason why traveling is so important. It takes seeds and other plant parts into new areas that are less crowded. There they have a better chance of surviving.

The traveling of plant parts to new areas is called *dissemination*. Dissemination does more than just prevent crowding. As plants grow, they change the environment around them. Sometimes, they change it so much that their own offspring cannot live there. White pine seedlings, for instance, require sunshine; but when they grow into adult trees, they shade the ground beneath them. A forest of white pine trees is too dark for good growth of its own seedlings. The seeds blown by the wind out of the forest and into a sunnier place have a much better chance of growing into adult trees. So dissemination also takes some plants away from places where they cannot grow well and takes them to places better suited to them.

The parts of plants that travel are called *disseminules*. Seeds and fruits are disseminules familiar to almost everyone. So, too, are some offshoots of adult plants like bulbs and corms. Stems, leaves, or roots may break off from a plant and travel to new places. Even entire plants, like tumbleweeds, can become uprooted from the ground; then, the wind can blow them about, their seeds dropping as they go.

Spores are disseminules so small that we usually do not notice them, but you can find them easily enough if you take the trouble to look for them. Each spore is a single cell no larger than the size of a speck of dust, but it can grow into an entire plant. Many ferns, mosses, algae, and fungi are disseminated by spores.

Regardless of their differences, disseminules have certain features in common:

    1. Each consists of living material. A spore is only one cell. Other disseminules may contain hundreds or thousands of cells.

    2. When it arrives in a suitable place, a disseminule can produce one or more complete plants.

    3. A disseminule contains enough food to keep itself alive for days, weeks, or even years and then to nourish the young plant that grows from it until it becomes large enough to produce its own food.

How do disseminules travel to new areas? Winds blow some of them to many places around the world. Rivers and ocean currents carry others. Some become stuck on the fur of animals and travel with them. Still others are eaten by animals and remain alive while they pass through the animals' digestive systems. A few plants even shoot their disseminules away.

Traveling
With the Wind

When a strong wind blows and the weather is dry, go outside and close your eyes. How many ways do you feel the wind?

Your clothes flutter in the breeze. Hold them tightly about you for a moment. Then open your coat or spread some item of clothing out as wide as you can and face into the wind. Notice how much more force the wind seems to have now.

Strong gusts tug at your hair and whip it about your head. The longer your hair, the harder it seems to be pulled.

Does the wind blow anything into your face? If there has been no rain for a long time, you might feel dust particles hitting your skin.

Look about you. What kinds of objects do not move with the wind? Heavy and bulky things like a baseball or a brick remain still in ordinary winds.

Can you imagine what might be the best shapes or sizes for disseminules that travel with the wind? Think about it as you read the following pages.

WINGED DISSEMINULES

Stand under a maple tree when its fruits are ripe and watch them flutter downward. Each fruit looks a little like two peanuts stuck together with two wings extending from opposite sides. Sometimes, the fruit breaks in half; then each half has only one wing.

The wings look like propellers, and they make the fruit twist about in the air, slowing its fall. On a calm day, most of the fruits land near the tree. But they can be carried on the wind. The stronger the breeze, the farther they are

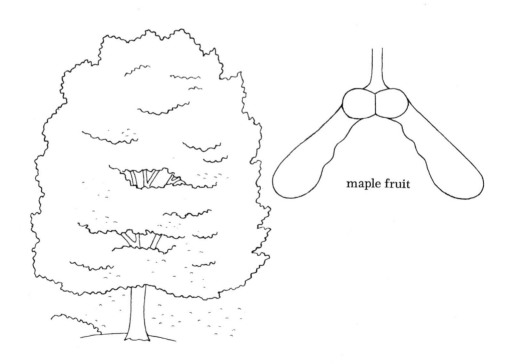

maple fruit

for another year, there comes a day when a snowdrift seems to cover my lawn, and snowflakes appear to fill the air. For a moment, I gaze in wonder, for the day is hot. Then I realize that the "snow" consists of seeds slowly drifting away from my neighbor's cottonwood tree. Each small seed bears a fuzzy tuft of hair like fine, white, cotton threads. Like the wings on maple fruits, the hairs of cottonwood seeds slow their descent and increase their chances of being blown away by a breeze; but, on calm days, most of them become entangled among the blades of grass in my lawn. On a windy day, however, the seeds swirl upward on the gusts that carry them beyond my sight. Some travel this way for many miles.

How many disseminules with hairs have you seen? Probably everyone knows dandelions. After their yellow blos-

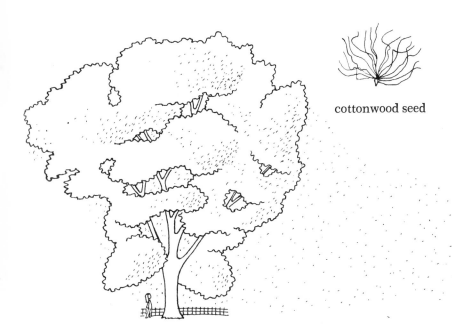

cottonwood seed

a winged seed:

pine

some winged fruits:

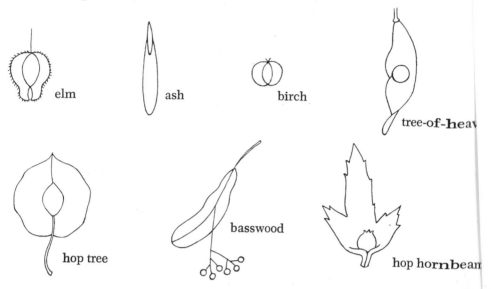

elm

ash

birch

tree-of-heav

hop tree

basswood

hop hornbeam

likely to travel, although only strong gusts will blow many of them more than a few hundred feet from the tree.

Most winged disseminules are produced by trees or climbing vines and very few by short plants. The higher the disseminule is before it begins to fall, the greater the chance of its being caught by a breeze.

Some other winged disseminules are the seeds of pine, spruce, hemlock, and the fruits of several other trees: elm, ash, birch, tree of heaven, hoptree, and hop hornbeam. Basswood trees produce fruits attached to a special leaf that acts as a wing. In each case, the wing enables the wind to blow the disseminule as it drops from the parent plant.

DISSEMINULES WITH HAIRS
Late in spring, when the cold weather of winter has gone

dandelion fruit

soms fade, tiny fruits appear in fluffy, round heads. Each fruit bears its own parachute made of fine hairs that keep it aloft in the wind. Nearly every child has picked a ripe dandelion head and used his own breath to provide it with a breeze. If you haven't already done this, try it the next time you see dandelions with fruits. Usually, you can find them from late spring well into autumn.

Have you ever noticed that the flowering stems of dandelions grow taller when they form fruits? This puts the fruits in a higher position where they are more likely to be caught by a breeze.

some seeds and fruits with hairs:

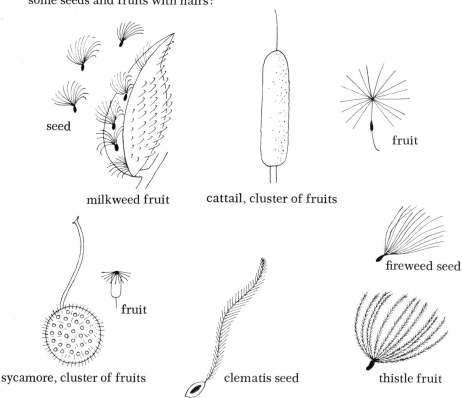

seed

milkweed fruit

cattail, cluster of fruits

fruit

fireweed seed

fruit

sycamore, cluster of fruits

clematis seed

thistle fruit

Some other disseminules with hairs are the seeds of milk-
weeds, willow trees, fireweeds, and the fruits of cattails,
sycamore trees, clematis, thistles, and goldenrods.

Generally, hairs enable seeds and fruits to travel for at
least several miles—sometimes, many miles. The wind can
carry them farther than it can winged disseminules.

MINUTE DISSEMINULES

Minute disseminules are so small that they look like powder
or dust. Most minute disseminules are spores. Not all spores
travel by air, but those of many fungi, mosses, and ferns do.
These single cells are blown about as easily as dust by the

wind. If they land in a suitable place, each one can grow into an entire plant. So easily does even the smallest breeze pick them up, that it does not matter if they form near the ground. Many mosses are not even an inch tall, and yet their spores travel far with the wind.

Because spores are so small, we usually do not notice them. As they travel in the air, they ordinarily are invisible. You can find them more easily if you have a plant that is producing them.

Have you ever made a spore print from a mushroom? A mushroom is one kind of fungus. It has a stalk and a cap. Get a mushroom—the edible kind you buy in the super-market will do very well—in which the bottom of the cap has separated from the stalk so that you can see the flat, brown gills in the cap. The gills radiate from the stalk the way the spokes radiate from the center of a wheel. The mushroom produces millions of spores on the sides of its gills.

Remove the stalk from the mushroom and place the cap, open side down, on a piece of white paper. Wait about 12 hours and then look under the cap. (If you use a wild mush-room collected fresh from a woods or field, 5 or 10 minutes

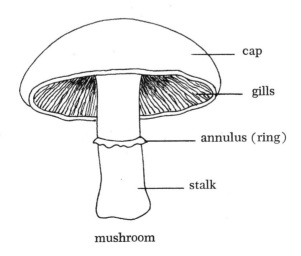

cap

gills

annulus (ring)

stalk

mushroom

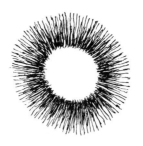

mushroom spore print

may be enough. If it has light-colored gills, put the cap on dark paper. Don't eat wild mushrooms unless you know they are edible. Some of them are very poisonous!) Spores falling from the gills onto the paper make a pattern. The lines of spores correspond to the spaces between the gills.

To learn just how light and powdery the spores are, rub your finger across the spore print. Some of the spores will come off on your finger, but they are so fine you probably will not be able to feel them. Neither are you likely to see individual spores with the unaided eye. You can see them as very small dots with a strong magnifying glass or hand lens.

Lay two pencils side by side about an inch apart on a piece of paper and set another mushroom cap on them. Even in a room with the doors and windows closed, the air moves gently, and some air will flow beneath the cap. Wait as long as you did for the other spore print. How does this one differ from the first one? How far do you think the spores would travel in a strong breeze?

Wind dissemination is efficient on dry days, but not on wet ones. Raindrops beat disseminules down to the ground. Water on them adds to their weight and makes them too heavy for the wind to lift. In the case of structures as fine as spores, water causes them to clump together, and the clumps become too heavy for the wind to pick up.

Mosses release their spores only in dry weather when they are light and separate easily from each other. The spores form in capsules on the tops of stalks. A lid on the capsule protects the developing spores from rain. In most kinds of mosses, the capsule bends downward when its spores are ripe and ready to be disseminated. The lid falls off, revealing a ring of triangular teeth surrounding the opening. In wet weather, the teeth fit tightly together with no space between them. This securely closes the capsule, and no spores can fall out. In dry weather, the teeth spread apart, and the spores sift out between them. As the spores fall downward, even the slightest breeze carries them away.

Minute disseminules often travel great distances. Winds may carry them several miles upward. There they can float for thousands of miles. Some travel half way around the world or farther. Ferns arrived on many oceanic islands this way. Some of these islands are hundreds or thousands

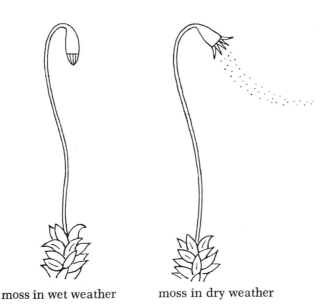

moss in wet weather   moss in dry weather

of miles away from other land. The first ferns to appear there grew from spores that traveled all that way by wind. Today, their offspring beautify the islands, and new spores arrive daily from other lands.

SHAPE, SIZE, AND THE WIND

Disseminules with wings, disseminules with hairs, disseminules so small that they can hardly be seen—these three look very different from each other. Yet all travel with the wind. What characteristics do they have in common that makes them easily blown by a breeze?

Generally, the wind moves most easily those objects that have a great deal of surface area compared to their weight. Because the wind blows against the surface of an object, the greater its surface area in contrast to its weight, the greater the chance that the wind can move it; in other words, heavy objects need more surface area than light ones to be blown by the same wind.

Things blown easily by the wind have a special shape or size that gives them extra surface area compared with their weight. Thin, flat objects, long hairs, and very tiny things generally have a great deal of surface area compared with their weight. The drawings and chart on page 19 help to show why this is so.

Remember feeling your flat clothes, your long hair, and the fine dust particles being blown by the wind? A baseball or a brick has a more compact shape than these objects; so, it does not have enough surface area for an ordinary wind to move it.

Plant disseminules that travel with the wind also have a large surface area compared with their weight. It is their

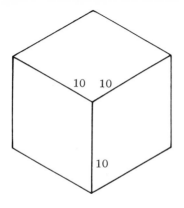

This is a cube. Each edge is 10 inches long. Let us assume that the cube weighs 1,000 ounces. The surface area of the cube is 600 square inches.

(10 x 10 x 6)

To get the ratio of its surface area to its weight, we divide its surface area by its weight:

$$\frac{600}{1000} = 0.6$$

We could compare this cube with a coconut or a brick, which is not moved by ordinary winds.

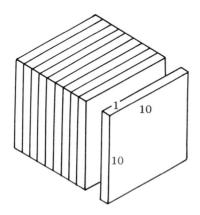

If the cube is cut into 10 flat pieces of equal size and shape, then each piece weighs 100 ounces. The surface area of each flat piece is 240 square inches.

$$10 \times 10 \times 2 = 200$$
$$1 \times 10 \times 4 = \underline{40}$$
$$240$$

The ratio of its surface area to its weight is

$$\frac{240}{100} = 2.4$$

Compare this flat object with winged disseminules or with your clothes. The flat shape gives it a higher ratio of surface area to weight, and so increases its chances of being blown by the wind.

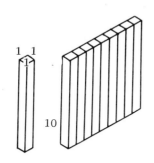

If one of the flat pieces is cut into 10 long pieces of equal size and shape, then each of these pieces weighs 10 ounces. The surface area of each long piece is 42 square inches.

$$1 \times 1 \times 2 = 2$$
$$1 \times 10 \times 4 = \underline{40}$$
$$42$$

The ratio of its surface area to its weight is

$$\frac{42}{10} = 4.2$$

Compare this long object with a hair. Its ratio of surface area to weight is greater than that of the flat object. A tuft of many hairs is more efficient for wind dissemination than a single wing.

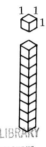

If one of the long pieces is cut into 10 equal cubes, then each of these small cubes weighs 1 ounce. The surface area of each of these small cubes is 6 square inches.

(1 x 1 x 6)

The ratio of its surface area to its weight is

$$\frac{6}{1} = 6$$

Compare this small cube with a minute disseminule or a speck of dust. Its ratio of surface area to weight is greater than that of the other objects on this page. Minute disseminules are the most easily carried by the wind.

wings, hairs, or minute size that gives them their large surface area. A tuft of many hairs made of the same kind and amount of material as a wing weighs the same as the wing, but it has a great deal more surface area. This is why hairs help disseminules to travel farther than wings do. Extremely small objects like spores have much more surface area compared to their weight than do either wings or hairs; so, they frequently travel the farthest of all wind-borne disseminules.

A great deal of surface area also slows the descent of a disseminule from the plant that produced it. On a calm day, the longer it takes a disseminule to fall to the ground, the better the chance that a breeze will come along and carry it away. You can test this easily. Take two identical pieces of paper—ordinary notebook paper is fine. Crumple one piece as tightly as you can. Both pieces weigh the same, but the crumpled piece now has less surface area exposed to the air. In a still room, hold both pieces as high as you can but at exactly the same height. Then drop them at the same time. Which one lands first?

Now repeat this experiment outside on a windy day. Which piece travels farther?

As you look at all kinds of wind-borne disseminules, try to imagine how far they will travel.

Traveling by Water

Have you ever seen water move things? Watch a stream for several minutes. If you don't live near a river, observe the water flowing in a gutter after a rain, instead. Does anything move downstream with the water? What kinds of things are they?

Can you see objects in the stream that do not move? What kinds of things are they?

If you live where the weather is always dry (or even if you don't), you might like to perform the following experiment:

Fill a large bowl with water about 3 inches deep. Take two small pieces of aluminum foil exactly the same size. Crumple one of them into a very loose ball so that there is

plenty of air inside it. Drop it in the water. Does it sink or float?

Now fold the other piece in half and press the two halves together so that there is no air between them. Fold it in half again and press it firmly again. Repeat this several times so that you have a very tightly packed piece of aluminum. Drop it in the water. Does it sink or float?

Now stir the water with your hand, so that you make a little current running around the bowl. Does either piece of aluminum move with the current you make?

Water moves most easily the things that float—the things that are lighter than water. Dry leaves, tree branches, a paper cup from someone's picnic lunch, wooden furniture, an empty can, a toy boat or a real one—big or small they float with the current.

Something heavier than water sinks to the bottom. Unless it is very small or the stream moves rapidly, it probably will stay where it sank and will not be moved downstream.

Aluminum is heavier than water, and so the tightly folded piece sinks. The crumpled piece floats because it contains air, and air is lighter than water. The floating piece of aluminum moves with a stream of water, but the sunken piece will not be moved by the gentle currents you are likely to make in a bowl.

Have you seen any other evidence that water moves things? During or after a rainstorm, find a place where rain falls on a patch of bare earth near a building. What happens to the side of the building? If rain is rare where you live, you can make your own with a garden hose. Or put a little damp soil in a bowl, place the bowl under a faucet, and open the faucet just enough to let the water fall drop by drop on the soil. What do you observe?

When raindrops fall, they hit the ground with enough force to move small objects. The side of the house or bowl becomes covered with mud as the falling drops splash tiny particles of soil up into the air. They land a few inches or a few feet away from their original location.

Very large things are not splashed away by falling drops of water, for the drops do not have sufficient force to move them.

You probably can guess now the characteristics of disseminules that travel by water. Most of them are lighter than water so they float with a current. And raindrops splash a few small disseminules about; some of these are large enough to be seen without the use of a magnifying glass—others are so small you would need a microscope to see them.

FLOATING DISSEMINULES

Many plants that live along the shores of rivers, ponds, lakes, and oceans have floating disseminules that fall into the water after they ripen. The water carries them to new shores where they may find suitable places to grow. Some disseminules travel only a few feet from the plant that produced them, and then they are washed up on the shore. Others float hundreds of miles downstream or across great distances of ocean.

The size of floating disseminules does not seem to matter much. Some are very small, others quite big. The most numerous plants of the oceans are microscopic algae that are carried thousands of miles by the currents. Coconut palms, that live in warm climates, produce some of the largest fruits known; and these fruits travel on ocean currents, too. Coconuts survive only short trips on ocean currents, however. Sea water slowly soaks into the seed and usually kills its embryo plant within a few days.

Large floating disseminules usually have air spaces that make them lighter than water. A coconut fruit is about the size of a football. The space between its woody outer shell and the hard inner shell that surrounds its big seed is

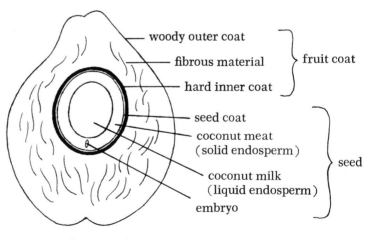

section of coconut fruit

loosely filled with coarse fibers. The air between the fibers keeps the fruit afloat in the sea, and enables it to travel to nearby islands. (The coconuts you usually see in the supermarkets are just the seeds surrounded by the hard inner shell of the fruit. The woody outer shell and nearly all of the fibrous material has been removed, but usually you can find a few of the fibers still clinging to it.) If waves carry a live coconut up onto a beach, the seed may sprout.

Of course, many aquatic plants have water-borne seeds and fruits. Water lilies, lotuses, waterweed (which you sometimes see in an aquarium), and water hyacinth are among them.

Fruits and seeds are not the only floating disseminules. If you place an onion or a clove of garlic in a bowl of water, you will see that these disseminules float. Some onion and garlic plants form small bulbs at the tops of stems where

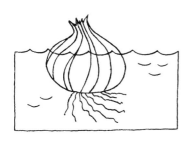

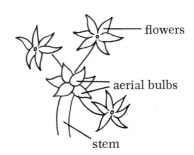

flowers

aerial bulbs

stem

onion plant producing aerial bulbs

you would expect to see flowers. When these bulbs fall into a pond or stream, they float to new places.

Bulbs of some other onion and garlic plants, as well as tulips and narcissus, form underground. So do corms like those of the crocus, gladiolus, and Chinese water chestnut. Because these disseminules are rich in food, small animals such as rats and muskrats enjoy eating them. When animals dig for bulbs or corms along a stream bank, they often knock a few into the water, which carries them away.

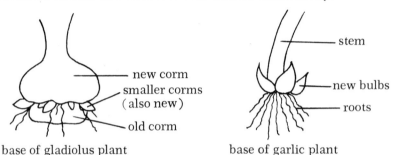

base of gladiolus plant   base of garlic plant

A volcano once helped biologists to learn how efficient dissemination by ocean currents is. In 1883, a volcanic eruption almost completely destroyed the island of Krakatoa in Indonesia. Only a part of the island remained, and the heat killed all the plants and animals that lived there. The nearest land from which new plants could come was an island 12 miles away. Fifteen years after the eruption, a biologist visiting the island found 53 kinds of seed plants living there. No one had brought them to Krakatoa. They came by natural means. About 60 percent of them had arrived by water-borne disseminules, about 32 percent came by air-borne disseminules, and only 8 percent had been brought by animals. So we see that water is an important means of travel for island plants.

SPLASH CUPS

When a water drop falls into a small cup, the drop breaks into smaller droplets, many of which splash out of the cup. If the cup contains small objects, these may be splashed out, too. A few plants produce small disseminules in cups called *splash cups*.

In the woods of northeastern and central parts of the United States lives a wild flower called bishop's-cap. Its fruits contain shiny, black seeds. When ripe, the fruits stand open and are small splash cups. Raindrops landing on a fruit splash its seeds several feet away. After a heavy rainstorm, nearly all the ripe fruits on a plant are empty.

Bishop's-cap fruits always stand upright. Even if something bends the plant into a horizontal position, the fruits slowly move back to their upright position. This way, they are most likely to receive raindrops.

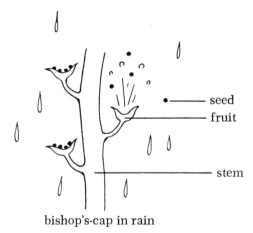

bishop's-cap in rain

SPRINGBOARDS

Have you ever watched a swimmer on a diving board? When he jumps on the board, what happens to it? First, it bends down under his weight; and then, it springs back up.

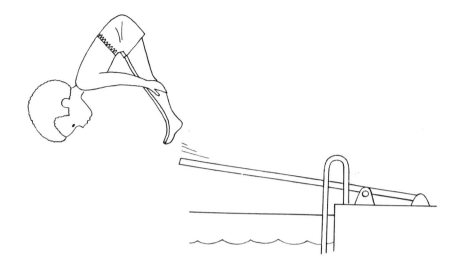

The upward movement of the board as he jumps up again gives the diver an extra push upward and lets him spring higher and farther than he would otherwise. Such a board is called a springboard. It bends easily, and it has one end securely attached to a firm support and a free end that can move up and down.

A few plants have springboards that toss disseminules several feet away from the plant. Raindrops operate these springboards.

When the lyre-leaved sage is in fruit, all that remains of the flower is a tube containing four small nutlets. The tube is open at one end. The closed end is attached to a small stem that grows from the main stem of the plant. The small stem is the springboard, and the tube with the nutlets is at its free end.

The nutlets do not fall out of the tube even if an animal or a strong wind shakes the plant vigorously from side to side. However, if something presses the tube downward so

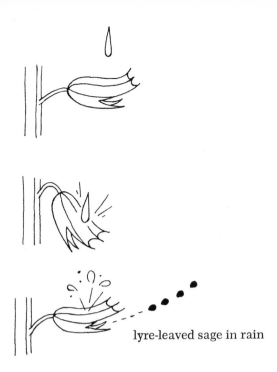

lyre-leaved sage in rain

that its stem becomes bent, when the stem springs back to its original position, it brings the tube up with enough force to shoot nutlets out of the tube. Some of them land 6 or more feet away from the plant. In nature, raindrops hitting the tube bend it down. In fact, the upper part of the tube has a cup-shaped depression just the right size for a large raindrop. A heavy rainstorm can disseminate many nutlets, for each sage plant produces many flowers.

Perhaps, you have seen the plant *Kalanchoë tubiflora* in florists' shops or greenhouses. This plant from Africa is a curiosity, for its narrow leaves bear several small plantlets along their edges. A small, strap-shaped stalk attaches each plantlet to a leaf. This stalk is the springboard, and a plantlet lies at its free end.

The force of a raindrop striking a plantlet bends the stalk down. When the stalk snaps back up, it tosses the plantlet away. Sometimes, plantlets fall 4 or 5 feet away from the parent plant. If they land in a favorable place, they take root and grow into adult plants.

Raindrops hitting springboards and splash cups do not carry disseminules nearly as far as strong ocean currents or streams do. Nevertheless, they do take disseminules far enough away from the parent plants so that the young plants are not crowded by the old ones, and this is important.

Kalanchoë leaf in rain

Traveling
With Animals

Some autumn day put on your oldest clothes and take a walk in a woods, meadow, or vacant lot. Do not stay on a path, but stroll among the trees and shrubs. (Don't go so far away from a path that you get lost.) Are there any seeds or fruits on your clothes? Examine some of them to see what makes them stick.

Put on your boots and walk in some mud by a pond or stream. When you get home, look closely at the mud on your boots. Can you find any disseminules in it? Do they differ from the ones that stuck to your clothes?

If you don't have a stream nearby, wait for a rainy day to find some mud. With your muddy boots, walk on an untended lawn or under a bird feeder with bird food scattered below it. Whenever your pet dog or cat comes home with muddy paws, examine them for disseminules.

What do you do with an apple core if you are on a picnic in the woods and there is no garbage can nearby?

How many ways do you think animals disseminate plants?

DISSEMINULES THAT CLING TO ANIMALS

Just as you can collect disseminules on your clothes without trying to do so, so animals can pick them up merely by brushing gently against some plants. Many dry fruits have spines, hooks, or barbs that become caught on the fur or feathers of passing animals. An animal carrying them may not even be aware of it, but he can carry them for many miles before they fall off.

Several kinds of beggar's-ticks grow throughout most of the United States. Their small, dry fruits grow in clusters at the tips of the stems. Each fruit has two or more narrow projections called *awns* pointing outward where they are most likely to touch a passing animal. Each awn has many fine barbs pointing backward. When the awns become caught in an animal's fur (or your woolen sweater), the little barbs prevent them from slipping back out. If you have ever had some of them on your clothes, you know how hard it is to remove them. You can imagine how long they would stay on an animal's fur. Many fruits are formed in

some fruits with awns, spines, hooks, or barbs:

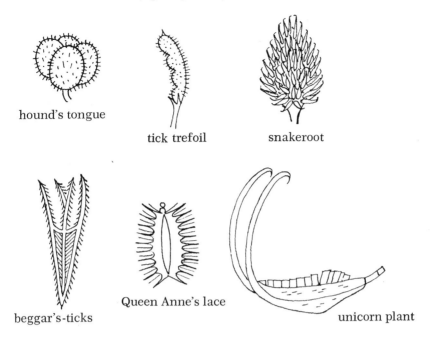

hound's tongue

tick trefoil

snakeroot

beggar's-ticks

Queen Anne's lace

unicorn plant

autumn when animals migrate; then, they can be carried long distances before they fall off.

Some other plants that produce fruits with spines, hooks, or barbs are tick trefoil, snakeroot, hound's-tongue, Queen Anne's lace, and the unicorn plant.

Even more difficult to remove from your clothes than beggar's-ticks are the burs of burdock. Each bur is a cluster of several dry fruits, and the cluster is surrounded by many hooked spines that become firmly attached to fur or clothes. Perhaps, your dog or cat has come home with tangled mats of them caught in his coat after an autumn day in a field or vacant lot. The individual fruits drop out of the bur one or two at a time. In this way, the fruits land in different places as the animal travels.

Some other burs are those of cocklebur, sandbur, and agrimony.

some burs with hooks or spines:

agrimony

cocklebur

sandbur

burdock

Sticky substances surround some disseminules and help to attach them to animals. Mistletoe has such seeds. It grows on tree branches in the southern part of the United States. It is a parasite that gets its food from the trees. Its roots grow into the tree branches and absorb food from the branch. Mistletoe cannot survive rooted in the ground like other plants. Therefore, only those seeds that land on tree branches will produce new mistletoe plants. This little plant produces small berries that birds enjoy eating. The berries contain sticky seeds that cling to the birds' bills as they eat. To wipe them off, the birds rub their bills against tree branches, and so they deposit the seeds in a good place for them to germinate.

A disseminule does not have to have hooks or be sticky itself to cling to animals. Almost any small disseminule that

falls on mud or becomes buried in it can be carried by animals. If you walked with muddy boots under a bird feeder, you probably found plenty of seeds in the mud clinging to your boots. Yet, if you examine the seeds, you will find that they are smooth. It was the mud that stuck them to your boots.

Mud clings to the feet of ducks, geese, and other shore birds walking along the muddy edge of a pond or stream. Any small disseminules in the mud are carried by the birds. If the birds fly to a nearby pond or stream, the mud may be washed off there. If they fly long distances, the mud may dry in flight and drop from their feet. In either case, the birds take disseminules to new areas.

EDIBLE DISSEMINULES

All disseminules contain some food, and many contain much more than the embryo needs to begin to grow. Because of this, animals find many of them good to eat.

In some cases, eating destroys the disseminule. If a squirrel opens a walnut and eats the meat inside, he eats the embryo. No plant will ever grow from that walnut. However, squirrels don't eat all the nuts they find. In autumn, they bury most of them and dig them up later as they need them. If a squirrel forgets about some of them, the next year they may sprout into new plants. In this case, the squirrel has not only disseminated the nuts, he has planted them as well.

Some trees planted this way are hickory, butternut, hazelnut, and oak. (Acorns are the nuts of oak trees.) The young horse chestnut trees in my yard grew from horse chestnuts that squirrels took from my neighbor's tree. Chipmunks, rats, and other rodents do this, too.

Eating seeds or fruits does not always kill the embryos in them. Juicy fruits such as cherries attract hungry animals. Some animals eat only the juicy part and let the seeds

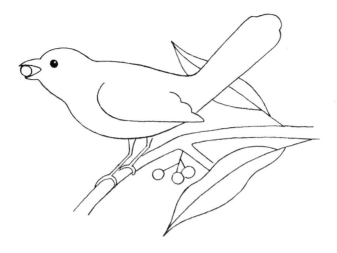

fall to the ground—just as you might absentmindedly throw away an apple core.

Other animals eat cherries whole. The cherry seed is surrounded by a hard covering that helps to protect the embryo inside it from the digestive juices of the animal. After the seed leaves the animal's body, the embryo is still alive, and the seed can germinate. Seeds of blackberries and strawberries also remain alive when the fruits are eaten.

HUMAN DISSEMINATORS

We must not forget that human beings are animals, too. Accidentally or on purpose, we disseminate plants all over the world.

When people move to a new area, they often take their favorite food plants and ornamental plants with them. If they like any of the plants they discover in their new homes, they may send them back to their friends and relatives living in their old homes.

After Columbus discovered America, Europeans who came here to live brought with them wheat, cabbage, beets, carrots, asparagus, and other crops. Corn, tomatoes, white and sweet potatoes, pumpkins, and squash were some of the new crops they discovered when they arrived in America.

People returning to Ireland took some white potatoes back with them, and there the potatoes grew so well that they soon became the major food crop of the country. Today, we even call them Irish potatoes, although they originally came from America.

How would you like spaghetti without tomato sauce? Before the discovery of America, that combination was not possible. Tomatoes grew only in America, and spaghetti was made in Europe from wheat, which grew there but not in the Western Hemisphere. Today, both tomatoes and wheat are grown in Europe and America, as well as other places where the weather and soil conditions are suitable. It was human beings who disseminated these plants.

Europeans also brought to America some of our most common weeds, including dandelions and Queen Anne's lace. So well do these plants grow here, you might think they had always been American weeds. People usually do not carry weeds about purposely, but the disseminules cling to the clothing of travelers or the hides of animals being shipped across oceans or continents. Some are hidden among crop seeds or in bales of hay to feed the animals being transported. So our trains, ships, and airplanes become disseminators, too.

Did you know that human beings are the only disseminators of a few plants? Corn grows only where farmers plant it in fields. As you know from eating corn on the cob, many kernels grow close together on an ear. The kernels do not drop off the ear one by one as they do from the stalks of other cereals like rice and wheat. If corn kernels should sprout on a fallen ear, their seedlings would be so crowded they soon would die. Birds, mice, and other animals eat corn, and sometimes they drop a few kernels that sprout, but this does not happen often enough for an entire field of corn to reproduce itself.

Over thousands of years, farmers have removed the husks from ears, collected the kernels, and saved some of them to plant the following year. Today, special corn breeders do this and sell the kernels to farmers for planting. If people did not continue to do this, we would have no more corn. There is no place that corn grows wild where we could get some more kernels.

Plants That Disseminate Themselves

Have you ever played tiddlywinks? Do you remember how to move a wink? You use one wink to squeeze another against the table on which you are playing. If you squeeze just right, the wink hops through the air.

Here's an experiment you might like to perform. You will need a piece of twine about 3 inches long, a little powder (or flour), and a dark-colored piece of paper. Fray one end of the twine and fluff it out. Then twist the whole piece of twine in the same direction that its individual threads are twisted (otherwise you will just unwind it). Keeping it twisted, dip the frayed end in the powder. Hold the twine with the frayed end down over the dark paper. Now let go of the frayed end. As the twine twists back to its original

shape, notice how the powder sprays over the paper.

Repeat this several times, sometimes twisting the twine more tightly, sometimes more loosely. Which way does the powder travel farthest?

Have you ever spit anything out of your mouth? It's not very polite, but you probably have done it. What do you do when you spit? To start with, you close your lips tightly. Then you force as much air into your mouth as you can. As more and more air comes in, it presses more and more strongly against all parts of your mouth. When you relax your lips a little bit, the air rushes out between them taking with it whatever you have in your mouth. Actually, you have created a small explosion.

Some plants that disseminate themselves toss their disseminules away by squeezing them, by twisting some part quickly, or by small explosions. Others merely grow into new areas.

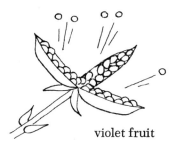

violet fruit

In summer, the fruit of the violet splits open into three sections shaped like little canoes. In each section lie two rows of small, round, black seeds. As the fruit dries, the two walls of a section move closer together and squeeze the seeds out one by one. Each seed pops up and lands a few inches or a few feet away.

The fruits of witch hazel shrubs squeeze their seeds out, too. If you live in the eastern half of the United States, you might look for this small tree in autumn. You can recognize it by its small, yellow flowers with four long petals. It probably will have yellow leaves at this time. Look for tan fruits about a third of an inch across. Take a twig with ripe fruits home with you. From time to time, you will hear the seeds hitting the wall as the fruits shoot them across the room.

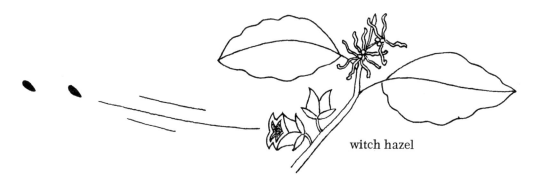

witch hazel

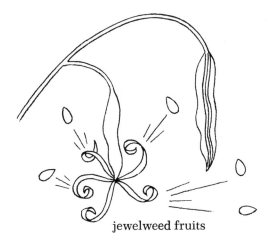

jewelweed fruits

TWISTING FRUITS

Touch-me-not is a good name for the wild flower some persons call jewelweed. Its fruits look like small pods about an inch in length. Each fruit is divided the long way into five sections. When completely ripe, the five sections separate from each other by coiling up rapidly. This quick movement tosses the seeds out of the sections. If the fruits are just ready to open, the slightest touch sets them off. That is why this plant is called touch-me-not.

If you should come upon this plant late in summer or autumn, take one of the fruits into your cupped hand. The splitting fruit will tickle it.

Sweet pea fruits are pods containing a row of seeds. They

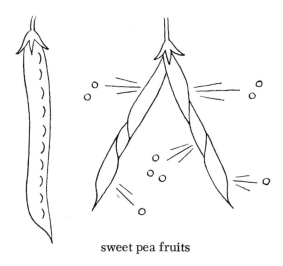

sweet pea fruits

look a little like green bean pods, but they ripen into strong, hard, dry fruits. Then suddenly, they split into two halves that twist tightly and toss the seeds several feet away.

DISSEMINATION BY EXPLOSION

You might say that the squirting cucumber spits out its seeds. The fruit looks something like a small pickle. As it ripens, water moves from the stem into the fruit. As more and more water enters, more and more pressure develops in the fruit. Then the ripe fruit falls from the plant. Its weakest point is the small part that was attached to the stem. This part bursts, and the contents of the fruit squirt out. The seeds may be carried as much as 20 feet away.

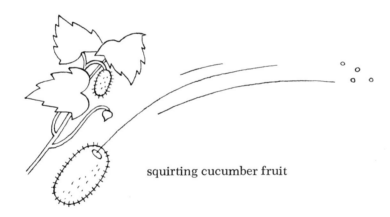

squirting cucumber fruit

PLANTS THAT GROW INTO NEW AREAS

The walking fern grows step by step into new places. You might not recognize it as a fern, for it does not look like most ferns. Its leaves are long, and they taper to a point.

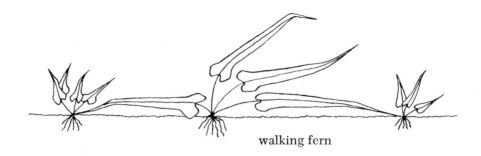

walking fern

As they grow larger, their tips bend over and touch the ground. Then new plantlets grow at the tips. The plantlets grow into independent plants, and soon their own leaves form plantlets the same way. Gradually, the older plants die, and the new ones become separated from each other. In this way, walking fern spreads into new places.

Strawberry plants spread in a similar way, but, in this case, it is the stem and not the leaf that forms new plants. Such stems are sometimes called *runners*, and they grow outward from the plant. When they touch the soil, new plants can form.

Some other plants that grow this way are irises, trailing arbutus, white potatoes, and many kinds of ferns and grasses. Their stems all grow along the surface of the ground or beneath it. Because these plants branch so much, you usually can cut their stems into several pieces and plant them separately. Then you have several plants. The same kind of thing happens naturally when the oldest parts of the stem die. Then its younger branches become separated from each other, and each forms a new plant.

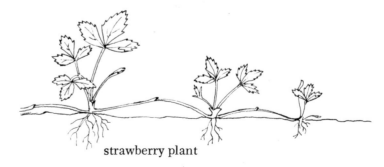

strawberry plant

Disseminules That Die

Not all disseminules arrive in places suitable for their growth. In fact, most of them do not.

On a calm day, the seeds of my neighbor's cottonwood tree fall directly below the tree. So many will there be that they may even accumulate in piles. None of them will produce new trees because they are in too crowded a place. On a windy day, some of the seeds may be blown into a lake or river where it is too wet for them, and they will die. Others may land in a rocky area that is too hot by day, too cold by night, and always too dry; here, they will die. Only those that find the right kind of soil, the right temperature, and the right amount of moisture will germinate.

Not even all those that germinate will grow into trees.

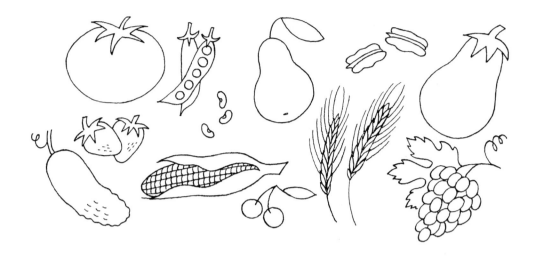

Some of the seedlings still may be too crowded to live long. Animals will eat some, and others will be trampled underfoot. Some may become diseased and die. A flood or a prolonged drought will kill others. Very few will ever become trees.

Because only a small portion of all disseminules can survive, plants must produce them in great abundance. Then it does not matter that many die. If my neighbor's cottonwood tree lives to be 100 years old, it will produce millions of seeds. If only one seedling from all those seeds lives to become an adult tree, the cottonwood tree will have reproduced itself.

Even though most disseminules do not grow into new plants, they do not go to waste. Animals use some of them as food. What disseminules of plants did you eat today? Tomatoes, peas, onions, watermelon, potatoes—how many more can you think of? If plants did not produce them in abundance, we would have less to eat.

Disseminules that do not germinate and that are not eaten usually die and decay. Even this is not a waste. A plant must get minerals from the soil to stay alive. Some of the minerals absorbed by the cottonwood tree go into its seeds. When the dead seeds decay, the minerals in them return to the soil and enrich it. The grass in my lawn uses some of the minerals from the cottonwood seeds and grows better because of them. The cottonwood seedlings that do survive may use the minerals from some that do not survive, too. So may the dandelions, clover, and any other plants growing on soil enriched by the death of the seeds. In this way, the dead seeds become part of growing plants.

Living or dead, disseminules help to make possible the continued life of plants and animals on the earth.

The Parts of Plants That Travel

some seeds shown approximately life size:

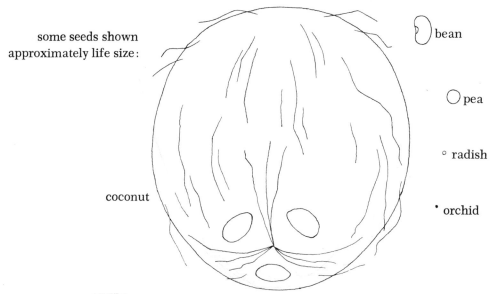

bean

pea

radish

orchid

coconut

SEEDS

Most seeds are small enough so that you can hold several of them in your hands easily. Some, like orchid seeds, are so tiny that you could hardly pick a single one up between your fingers. A few, like coconuts, are so large that just one is a handful.

A seed contains within it an embryo plant. Like an adult plant, the embryo usually has a root, a stem, and at least one leaf. If you open a squash or pumpkin seed, you will find an embryo filling the inside. It has two special seed leaves called *cotyledons*. The pointy end of the embryo is its root. Gently separate the cotyledons. If you look closely, you will barely be able to see a very small stem tip between

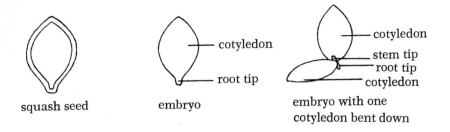

squash seed embryo embryo with one
cotyledon bent down

them. If a seed lands in a suitable place, its embryo will
grow into an adult plant. When the embryo begins to grow
and emerges from the seed, we say the seed *germinates*.

The embryo needs food not only while it travels, but also
when it sprouts into a young seedling. Some embryos contain all their food within their bodies, especially in the cotyledons. This is true of squash, pumpkins, beans, and peas.
Some other embryos get nourishment from a tissue in the
seed called *endosperm*. More than half of a corn seed consists of endosperm. When you eat breakfast cereals made
from corn, wheat, rice, or oats, you eat mostly endosperm.

You can even drink one kind of endosperm—coconut
milk. The small coconut embryo lies embedded in the outer
solid endosperm; this is the white coconut meat that we enjoy shredded in candy bars, cakes, and cookies. Liquid endosperm fills the center of the seed; this coconut milk makes
a refreshing drink on a hot afternoon.

A seed coat surrounds the embryo—and the endosperm,
if the seed has one. Some seed coats are hard and firm and
protect their embryos from drying out and from mechanical
damage. They also discourage insects that might otherwise
eat the embryos, and they guard against infection by bac-
teria and fungi.

You might like to watch some seeds produce new plants.
Any kind of seed you can buy in a garden shop will do. Soak
a paper towel in water, then fold it and place it in the bot-

tom of a glass jar. If your seeds are small (like radish or snapdragon seeds), just sprinkle a dozen or so on the wet paper, and then set the cover loosely on the jar. If the seeds are somewhat larger (like beans or peas), they will sprout faster if you soak them in water for a few hours or overnight before placing them on the wet paper. Add a little water every day—just enough to keep the towel wet, but not enough to cover the seeds. Within a few days, roots will grow from the seeds. In a few more days, leaves and stems will appear.

If you want to watch your seedlings grow into adult plants, transplant them to soil in a flowerpot or garden.

FRUITS

A fruit develops from a *pistil,* which is the female part of a flower. Each pistil has three parts: *stigma* (the upper part), *style* (the middle part), and *ovary* (the lower, swollen part). If the stigma receives pollen, the ovary may ripen into a fruit. Each fruit contains one or more seeds.

If you cut open an orange or a lemon, you will see that the fruit is divided into several sections, each containing

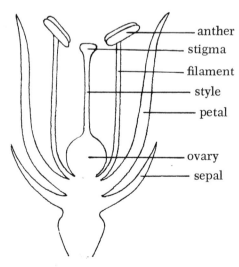

parts of a flower

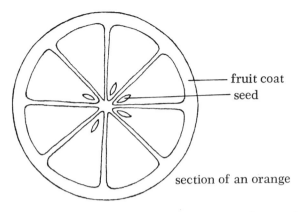

fruit coat
seed

section of an orange

several seeds. The outer wall of the fruit protects the seeds.

If its seeds are not released from a fruit while it is still on the plant, then the fruit may be the disseminule—that is, the entire fruit with its seeds still inside travels. For instance, a squirrel may carry an entire apple containing ten seeds away from a tree. The seeds will be released when the squirrel or some other animal eats the fruit or when the fruit decays.

Not all fruits are as juicy as oranges or apples. Bean pods and pea pods are fruits, too. If you open one of these pods, you will see that it is not divided into several sections but has only one cavity. It does have several seeds, however.

Sunflower "seeds" are not really seeds, but dry fruits called *achenes*. You can shell a sunflower achene by cracking the outer fruit coat. Inside is a loose seed with a very thin seed coat. Peel away the seed coat, and you will find an embryo very much like that of the pumpkin seed described in the Seeds section above.

Other "seeds" that really are fruits are the kernels of corn, wheat, rice, and oats. Each kernel is a one-seeded fruit; the seed and fruit are so firmly attached to each other that you cannot shell them easily like achenes. It is easy to see why so many persons call them seeds.

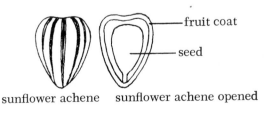

fruit coat

seed

sunflower achene   sunflower achene opened

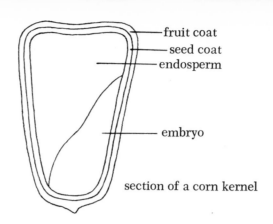

- fruit coat
- seed coat
- endosperm

- embryo

section of a corn kernel

Most nuts are fruits, too. You usually can open an acorn with a nutcracker. Inside the hard fruit coat, a papery seed coat surrounds the embryo with its two enormous cotyledons.

Hard, dry fruit coats protect the seeds inside them. This is especially important if the seed coats are thin—as they are in sunflower achenes and acorns.

If you like, soak some sunflower achenes or corn kernels in water and set them on a wet paper towel in a jar. In a few days, young seedlings will come from them.

OFFSHOOTS

Offshoots are stems, roots, or leaves that grow outward from a parent plant and then become detached from it. An animal may remove the offshoot, the parent plant may die, or some tissue connecting the offshoot to the parent plant may die.

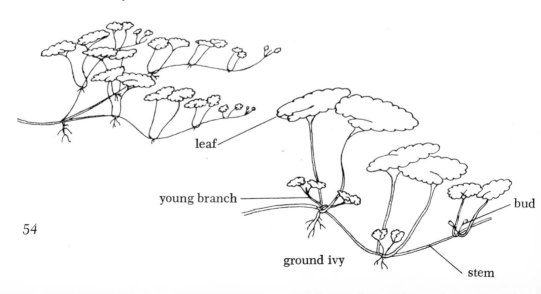

leaf

young branch

bud

ground ivy

stem

Stems that function as offshoots have their own leaves and buds as other stems do. Roots usually grow from them —if not before they are detached, then soon afterward. Perhaps you have cut a stem from an ivy or geranium plant and watched roots grow from it.

Except for a flower bud, each bud on such a stem is really a very short stem with its own leaves and small buds. A bud can open and grow into a larger stem; later, its own buds can do the same thing. In this way, stem offshoots may spread into new territory.

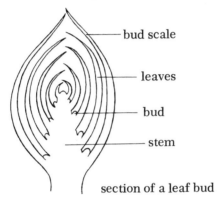

bud scale

leaves

bud

stem

section of a leaf bud

Some stem offshoots have special names. The stems of strawberries grow horizontally above the ground and are called *stolons*. Many ferns and grasses have *rhizomes*, stems that grow horizontally at the surface of the ground or beneath it. Tubers are enlarged portions of rhizomes. White potatoes are tubers.

Only a few roots and leaves can act as disseminules. If they become separated from a plant, most roots and leaves die. Dandelion roots are among the few that can form their own buds, and from them, new stems and leaves develop. When a leaf of a *Bryophyllum* plant falls to the ground,

Bryophyllum leaf with young plants

young plantlets form along its edges. As the plantlets grow bigger, the old leaf dies.

A *bulb* is really a large bud that stores food. It consists mostly of leaves. These leaves are attached to a short, upright stem at the base of the bulb. Cut an onion bulb in half from top to bottom, and you will see thick white leaves coming from a stem. These leaves store most of the food in the bulb. The papery leaves on the outside help to protect the inner ones from drying out. Roots grow down from the bottom of the stem. The onions you buy in a store may have no roots, but, usually, they have at least some small, dry ones.

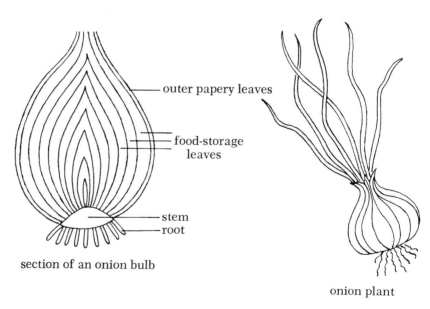

outer papery leaves

food-storage leaves

stem
root

section of an onion bulb

onion plant

Some other plants that produce bulbs are tulips, narcissus, hyacinths, and garlic. The garlic bulbs that you buy in the grocery store are really clusters of little bulbs called "cloves."

When a bulb becomes detached from a plant, animals or water may carry it about. If it reaches a suitable place, fresh roots develop from the bottom, and a stem and leaves emerge from the top. For a winter flower arrangement, some people plant narcissus bulbs among pebbles in a shallow dish with a little water. In a few weeks, the bulbs produce blooming plants.

Corms are much like bulbs, but they consist mostly of short, thick, firm stems with only a few papery leaves on the outside. In this case, the stem and not the leaves stores the food. You might like to plant crocus or gladiolus corms and watch them sprout into new plants.

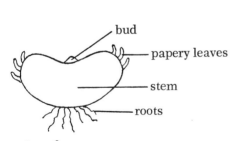

section of a crocus corm

crocus plant in bloom

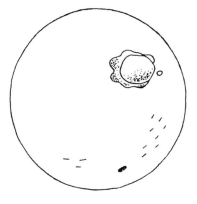

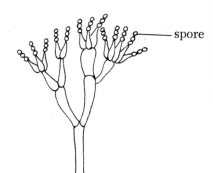
spore

orange with green mold

small portion of green mold
much enlarged

SPORES

Spores are disseminules composed of only a single cell
containing enough food to keep the cell alive. Spores contain no embryos or endosperm; nor do they have stems,
leaves, or roots in them. Most spores are so small that you
could not see an isolated one without a microscope. Yet a
spore can develop into a complete plant if it arrives in a
place suitable for its growth. Many algae, fungi, mosses,
and ferns travel mainly by spores. These plants produce no
seeds or fruits, and except for the ferns, they have no stems,
roots, or leaves.

Perhaps you have seen a green mold with a white edge
growing on very ripe fruits. The green portion consists of
thousands or even millions of green spores. You can rub
some of them off easily with your fingers, but it is hard to
see a single one. The white portion of the mold is the young-
est part, which has not yet formed spores.